SARINA JACOBSON
APPLES
More Than 75 Delicious Recipes

PHOTOGRAPHY BY DANYA WEINER

STERLING

New York / London
www.sterlingpublishing.com

CONTENTS

INTRODUCTION 6

Types of Apples 6

Selecting and Storing 7

Slicing and Cooking 7

Nutritional Information 7

SOUPS 8

Curried Apple Lentil Soup 10

Chestnut and Apple Soup 12

Chilled Apple Soup 13

Carrot, Apple, and Ginger Soup 14

Apple, Celery, and Celeriac Soup 16

Beet, Feta, and Apple Soup 17

Watercress and Apple Soup 18

Pumpkin and Apple Soup 20

Country-Style Vegetable and Apple Soup 21

SALADS 22

Grilled Apple and Chicken Salad 24

Spinach, Apple, and Wheat Berry Salad 26

Quinoa and Apple Salad 28

Fruit and Nut Salad 29

Smoked Salmon and Apple Salad 30

Roasted Apple and Beet Salad 32

Spicy Apple, Brie, and Rice Salad 34

Thai-Style Green Apple Salad 35

Apple, Chicken, and Wasabi Salad 36

BREADS, MUFFINS, AND COOKIES 38

Apple and Pumpkin Loaf 40

Chocolate Chip Apple Cookies 40

Cranberry-Apple Loaf 42

Apple and Spice Muffins 44

Apple, Lemon, and Poppy Seed Muffins with Mint Syrup 46

Apple and Date Loaf 48

Orange, Apple, and Cranberry Muffins 49

Carrot and Apple Muffins 50

Apple Blondies 52

Apple, Date, and Ginger Muffins 54

Apple and Date Spice Cookies 55

Apple Oatmeal Cookies 56

Chocolate-Coated Apple Cranberry Cookies 58

Apple Muesli Cookies 60

CHICKEN AND MEAT 62

Roasted Chicken with Caramelized Fennel and Apples 64

Citrus Ginger Chicken 66

Chicken and Apple Tagine 67

Lemon, Apple, and Sage Grilled Chicken 68

Beef and Apple Stir-Fry 70

Apple and Sage Burgers with Caramelized Onions 72

Fruity Meatball Casserole 72

Cranberry-Apple Chicken 73

Apple and Spice Chicken 74

Lamb Chops with Caramelized Apples, Onions, and Mint 76

Easy Beef and Apple Curry 78

Braised Beef with Red Wine, Cranberries, and Apples 79

Pot Roast with Glazed Apple and Pears 80

CAKES, TARTS, PIES, AND OTHER DESSERTS 82

Apple Berry Crumble Cake 84

Rustic Apple Cake 86

Lemon Apple Cheesecake 88

Apple and Almond Tartlets 90

Apple Carrot Cake with Ginger Cream 92

Apple Upside-Down Cake 93

Apple Custard Tartlets 94

Classic Apple Pie 96

Mini Apple Crisps 98

Easy Tarte Tatin 100

Apple and Coconut Pudding 100

Easy Apple Strudel 101

Buttermilk Pancakes with Apples and Pecans 102

Mini Toffee Apple Puddings 104

Mini Apple Custard Pots 106

Apple and Plum Cake 108

BEVERAGES AND CONDIMENTS 110

Apple Champagne 112

Warm Apple Wine 112

Fruity Hot Cider 114

Apple Salsa 114

Mango-Apple Chutney 116

Apricot, Apple, and Pecan Stuffing 117

Apple Butter 118

Apple, Pineapple, Ginger, and Mint Smoothie 118

Apple Cider Dressing 120

Apple, Lemon, and Yogurt Smoothie 120

Applesauce 122

Simple Apple and Date Spread 122

Apple Cider Sauce 123

Apple Relish 123

Classic Apple Chutney 124

Apple Marmalade 126

Mushroom, Sage, and Apple Stuffing 126

INDEX 128

INTRODUCTION

Apple trees likely originated in Eastern Europe and southwestern Asia, but they are now cultivated in most temperate regions of the world. Over the centuries, many hybrids and cultivars have been developed, and there are now about 7,500 varieties of apples.

The apple is a member of the rose family. It has a compartmentalized core that classifies it as a pome, a category of fruit whose name derives from the Latin word for apple: *pomum*. Apples have crisp white flesh and various shades of red, yellow, or green skin. As for taste, apples may be sweet or tart. Golden and Red Delicious apples, for example, are among the sweeter varieties; Braeburn and Fuji apples are slightly tart; Gravenstein, Granny Smith, and Pippin apples are notably tart. Tart apples generally retain their texture during cooking and are often preferred for desserts such as apple pie. Sweet apples are usually best when eaten raw.

TYPES OF APPLES
The type of apple you choose depends upon your personal taste, and the intended use of the apple, but here are some general guidelines about which apples are usually preferred in various situations.

Fresh: McIntosh, Cortland, Jonathan, Red Delicious, Golden Delicious, Stayman Winesap, Melrose, Franklin, Prima, Braeburn, Fuji

Applesauce: Golden Delicious, Melrose, Yellow Transparent, McIntosh, Cortland, Jonathan, Grimes Golden, Stayman Winesap, Rome Beauty, Lodi

Baking: Cortland, Jonathan, Grimes Golden, Melrose, Rome Beauty, Yellow Transparent, Lodi, McIntosh, Golden Delicious, Stayman Winesap

SELECTING AND STORING

When selecting apples, look for firm fruit with rich coloring. For yellow or green varieties, a slight blush of color is said to be best. Look for smooth skin and few or no bruises. Bruising may be a sign that the apple is rotten.

Apples are best stored in a cool, dry place. Though a cold cellar is excellent, a refrigerator is fine, too. Simply place the apples (unwashed) in a plastic bag or store them in the crisper drawer. Check them regularly and remove any apples that show signs of decay. The old adage is true: one rotten apple can, indeed, spoil the lot! Do not freeze apples, since this bursts their cells and causes immediate damage.

SLICING AND COOKING

Apples start turning brown after they've been sliced. To prevent this, dip cut pieces of apple in apple cider or fruit juice (lemon, orange, pineapple, or grapefruit) before use. If you're cooking with apples, it is best to prepare them at the last minute. Peel, slice, or grate them just before mixing them with other ingredients so they do not discolor.

NUTRITIONAL INFORMATION

Apples are a good source of dietary fiber, and they contain vitamins A and C, potassium, and pectin. Most of the apple's fiber is contained in its skin, as are the majority of its flavonoids. Unfortunately, the skin of commercially grown apples is also the part most likely to contain pesticide or toxic residues. Since peeling dispenses with the apple's flavonoids and most of its valuable fiber, organic or unsprayed apples are preferable.

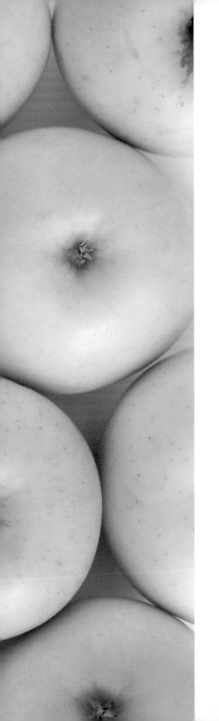

SOUPS

CURRIED APPLE LENTIL SOUP

The apple flavor complements the curry element in this hearty soup.
Serve with your favorite flatbread.

INGREDIENTS

Serves 4 to 6

1 tablespoon canola oil

1 tablespoon butter

1 medium onion, finely chopped

1 leek, finely chopped

1 medium carrot, peeled and coarsely chopped

2 celery stalks, finely chopped

1 tablespoon Indian curry paste

1 teaspoon sugar

2 medium sweet potatoes, peeled and coarsely chopped

2 medium Golden Delicious apples, peeled, cored, and coarsely chopped

¾ cup green-brown lentils, rinsed and drained

⅛ cup barley, rinsed and drained

One 8-ounce can chopped tomatoes, with juices

2 cloves garlic, crushed

8 cups chicken, beef, or vegetable stock

Salt and freshly ground black pepper

PREPARATION

1. In a large heavy-based saucepan, heat oil and butter over medium heat until butter melts. Add onion, leek, carrot, and celery, and sauté for about 3 minutes, or until onion and leek are transparent.

2. Stir in curry paste, sugar, sweet potatoes, apples, lentils, and barley, and cook over medium-high heat for 3 minutes.

3. Add tomatoes, garlic, and soup stock, increase heat to high, and bring to a boil. Immediately reduce heat to medium-low, cover, and simmer for about 1 hour, stirring occasionally, until barley is tender. Season with salt and pepper, and serve hot.

CHESTNUT AND APPLE SOUP

If you have the time, freshly roast the chestnuts for this recipe, as the aroma simply can't be beat. If you're in a rush, though, feel free to use pre-roasted chestnuts.

INGREDIENTS

Serves 4

1 pound raw chestnuts

4 cloves garlic, unpeeled

1 tablespoon extra-virgin olive oil

1 tablespoon butter

1 small onion, finely chopped

1 leek, finely chopped

1 carrot, peeled and finely chopped

1 celery stalk, finely chopped

4 sprigs fresh thyme

2 bay leaves

4 cups chicken, beef, or vegetable stock

1 cup applesauce

⅛ teaspoon ground nutmeg

2 tablespoons finely chopped fresh mint

Salt and freshly ground black pepper

PREPARATION

1. Preheat oven to 450°F. Line a baking sheet with parchment paper.

2. Cut an X into each chestnut shell. Arrange chestnuts and garlic on baking sheet, and roast for 20 to 30 minutes, or until chestnut shell begins to pull away from chestnut, and garlic is soft.

3. While chestnuts are still hot, remove outer shell and inner skin, and discard. Place chestnut flesh in a large bowl, squeeze in garlic pulp, and set aside.

4. In a large heavy-based saucepan, heat oil and butter over medium-high heat until butter melts. Add onion, leek, carrot, celery, thyme, and bay leaves, and sauté for about 3 minutes, or until onion and leek are transparent.

5. Add chestnuts, garlic, and soup stock; increase heat to high and bring to a boil. Immediately reduce heat to medium-low and simmer, covered, for 10 to 15 minutes, or until vegetables are tender. Remove from heat, discard thyme and bay leaves, and let cool.

6. Transfer to a food processor or blender (transfer in batches, if necessary), and blend until smooth. Pour into a clean saucepan, and stir in applesauce, nutmeg, and mint; season with salt and pepper. Reheat over medium-low heat, and serve hot.

CHILLED APPLE SOUP

*With apples, lime, and ginger, this light and refreshing soup is ideal for serving
on a summer evening, with crispy breadsticks or Melba toast.*

INGREDIENTS

Serves 4

2 tablespoons butter

1 leek, finely chopped

1 cup apple juice

4 medium Golden Delicious
apples, peeled, cored, and
finely chopped

2 soft medium Bosc pears,
peeled, cored, and finely
chopped

1 whole nutmeg

1 small cinnamon stick

2 tablespoons freshly
squeezed lime or lemon juice

1 tablespoon finely grated lime
or lemon rind

1 tablespoon ginger paste or
minced fresh ginger

2 cups plain yogurt

1 cup water

1 cup heavy cream

Handful fresh mint leaves, for
garnish

PREPARATION

1. In a medium heavy-based
saucepan, heat butter over
medium heat until melted. Add
leek and sauté for about 3
minutes, or until transparent.

2. Add apple juice, apples, pears,
nutmeg, and cinnamon. Increase
heat to high and bring to a boil.
Immediately reduce heat to
medium-low and simmer,
covered, for 10 to 15 minutes, or
until fruit is soft. Remove from
heat and let cool.

3. In the meantime, in a large
bowl, whisk together lime juice,
lime rind, ginger, yogurt, water,
and cream until well combined.

4. Discard nutmeg and
cinnamon, and transfer soup to a
food processor or blender
(transfer in batches if necessary).
Blend until smooth.

5. Pour fruit mixture into cream
mixture, and stir thoroughly.
Cover with plastic wrap and
refrigerate for at least 4 hours
before serving, or until
thoroughly chilled. Transfer to
individual bowls and garnish with
mint before serving.

CARROT, APPLE, AND GINGER SOUP

This soup has a wonderfully tangy flavor and a rich, beautiful color.
Serve with warm crusty bread.

INGREDIENTS

Serves 4

2 tablespoons butter

1 leek, finely chopped

2 celery stalks, finely chopped

3 large carrots, peeled and finely chopped

2 large parsnips, peeled and finely chopped

3 Golden Delicious apples, peeled, cored, and finely chopped

2 teaspoons ginger paste or minced fresh ginger

¼ teaspoon ground nutmeg

2 tablespoons finely grated orange rind

½ teaspoon dried chile flakes, plus more for garnish

4 cups chicken or vegetable stock

One 13-ounce can coconut cream

2 tablespoons finely chopped cilantro

2 tablespoons finely chopped fresh mint

Salt and freshly ground black pepper

Handful fresh cilantro leaves, for garnish

PREPARATION

1. In a large heavy-based saucepan, heat butter over medium heat until melted. Add leek and celery, and sauté for about 3 minutes, or until leek is transparent.

2. Stir in carrots, parsnips, apples, ginger, nutmeg, orange rind, and chile flakes. Add soup stock, increase heat to high, and bring to a boil. Immediately reduce heat to medium-low and simmer, covered, for about 20 minutes, or until vegetables and apples are tender. Remove from heat and let cool.

3. Transfer soup to a food processor or blender (transfer in batches if necessary), and blend until smooth. Pour into a clean saucepan, and mix in coconut cream, cilantro, and mint; season with salt and pepper. Heat over medium-high heat, stirring occasionally, until hot. Transfer to individual bowls and garnish with cilantro and chile flakes before serving.

APPLE, CELERY, AND CELERIAC SOUP

This healthy soup features the refreshing combination of apples and celery.
Serve with your favorite cheese bread.

INGREDIENTS

Serves 4

2 tablespoons butter

3 celery stalks, finely chopped

1 pound celeriac, peeled and finely chopped

1 medium onion, finely chopped

4 Granny Smith apples, peeled, cored, and cubed

5 cups vegetable stock

2 large bay leaves

4 tablespoons heavy cream

Salt and freshly ground black pepper

2 tablespoons finely chopped chives, for garnish

PREPARATION

1. In a large heavy-based saucepan, heat butter over medium heat until melted. Add celery, celeriac, and onion, and sauté for about 3 minutes, or until onion is transparent.

2. Mix in apples, soup stock, and bay leaves. Increase heat to high and bring to a boil. Immediately reduce heat to medium-low, and simmer, covered, for about 20 minutes, or until vegetables and apples are tender. Remove from heat and let cool.

3. Transfer soup to a food processor or blender (transfer in batches if necessary), and blend until smooth. Pour soup into a clean saucepan, add cream, and season with salt and pepper. Reheat over medium heat, stirring occasionally, until hot. Transfer to individual bowls and garnish with chives before serving.

BEET, FETA, AND APPLE SOUP

*With feta cheese and apples, this earthy soup features a wonderful combination
of flavors. Serve with crusty bread.*

INGREDIENTS

Serves 4

1 tablespoon extra-virgin
olive oil

1 medium onion, finely
chopped

1 pound (3 or 4 medium)
beets, peeled and grated

One 16-ounce can pureed
tomatoes

1 clove garlic, crushed

1 medium carrot, peeled and
grated

3 Golden Delicious apples,
peeled, cored, and grated

5 cups beef, vegetable, or
chicken stock

2 sprigs fresh thyme

Salt and freshly ground black
pepper

1 cup crumbled feta cheese,
for garnish

2 tablespoons finely chopped
chives, for garnish

PREPARATION

1. In a large heavy-based
saucepan, heat oil over medium
heat. Add onion and sauté for
about 3 minutes, or until onion
is transparent.

2. In a medium bowl, combine
beets, tomatoes, garlic, carrot,
and apples. Transfer to saucepan,
and add soup stock and thyme;
season with salt and pepper.
Increase heat to high and bring
to a boil. Immediately reduce
heat to medium-low and simmer,
covered, for about 20 minutes,
or until vegetables and apples are
tender. Remove from heat and
let cool.

3. Discard thyme, transfer soup
to a food processor or blender
(transfer in batches if necessary),
and blend until smooth. Pour
soup into a clean saucepan, and
reheat over medium heat, stirring
occasionally, until hot. Transfer to
individual bowls and garnish with
cheese and chives before serving.

WATERCRESS AND APPLE SOUP

This luxuriously green and healthy light soup is suitable for serving at any time of year.

INGREDIENTS

Serves 4 to 6

4 tablespoons butter

2 large bunches watercress, stems removed and chopped

2 leeks, finely chopped

½ pound potatoes, peeled and finely chopped

3 Granny Smith apples, peeled, cored, and finely chopped

Salt and freshly ground black pepper

5 cups vegetable or chicken stock

¼ cup sour cream

2 tablespoons finely chopped fresh mint

Olive oil, for garnish

PREPARATION

1. In a large heavy-based saucepan, heat butter over medium heat until melted. Add watercress, leeks, potatoes, and apples, and stir while sautéing until well coated in butter. Season with salt and pepper, reduce heat to low, and cover. Let vegetables cook for 20 minutes, stirring thoroughly after about 10 minutes.

2. Add soup stock, increase heat to high, and bring to a boil. Reduce heat to medium-low and simmer, covered, for 15 to 20 minutes, or until vegetables are tender. Remove from heat and let cool.

3. Transfer soup to a food processor or blender (transfer in batches if necessary), and blend until smooth. Pour soup into a clean saucepan, and stir in sour cream and mint. Reheat over medium-high heat, stirring occasionally, until hot. Transfer to individual soup bowls, and drizzle with oil before serving.

PUMPKIN AND APPLE SOUP

Pumpkin soup is open to many variations. In this version, the apple pairs well with the pumpkin and sweet potato. Serve with your favorite bread and cheese.

INGREDIENTS

Serves 4

1 tablespoon canola oil

1 tablespoon butter

1 medium onion, finely chopped

1 tablespoon ginger paste or minced fresh ginger

½ teaspoon ground cinnamon

½ teaspoon ground nutmeg

1 pound pumpkin, peeled and finely chopped

½ pound sweet potatoes, peeled and finely chopped

3 Granny Smith apples, peeled, cored, and finely chopped

3 cups chicken or vegetable stock

Salt and freshly ground black pepper

2 cups heavy cream

1 tablespoon finely grated orange rind

⅓ cup crushed shelled pumpkin seeds, for garnish

PREPARATION

1. In a large heavy-based saucepan, heat oil and butter over medium heat until butter melts. Add onion, ginger, cinnamon, and nutmeg, and sauté for about 3 minutes, or until onion is transparent.

2. Add pumpkin, sweet potatoes, apples, and soup stock; season with salt and pepper. Increase heat to high, and bring to a boil. Immediately reduce heat to medium-low and simmer, covered, for about 25 minutes, or until vegetables and apples are tender. Remove from heat; stir in cream and orange rind, and let cool.

3. Transfer soup to a food processor or blender (transfer in batches if necessary), and blend until smooth. Pour soup into a clean saucepan and heat over medium-high heat, stirring occasionally, until hot. Transfer to individual bowls and garnish with pumpkin seeds before serving.

COUNTRY-STYLE VEGETABLE AND APPLE SOUP

This chunky vegetable soup makes a hearty meal all on its own.

INGREDIENTS

Serves 4

1 tablespoon butter

1 tablespoon olive oil

2 medium onions, coarsely chopped

6 celery stalks, coarsely chopped

¼ cup finely chopped celery leaves

¼ cup finely chopped parsley

4 ounces canned pumpkin

1 medium carrot, peeled and coarsely chopped

1 medium potato, peeled and coarsely chopped

1 small sweet potato, peeled and coarsely chopped

1 medium zucchini, coarsely chopped

½ cup barley

1 large Granny Smith apple, peeled, cored, and coarsely chopped

5 cups vegetable, beef, or chicken stock

1 teaspoon ground cumin

1 teaspoon paprika

1 teaspoon ground coriander

Salt and freshly ground black pepper

PREPARATION

1. In a large heavy-based saucepan, heat butter and oil over medium heat until butter melts. Add onions, celery, celery leaves, parsley, pumpkin, carrot, potato, sweet potato, zucchini, barley, and apple, and sauté for about 3 minutes, or until onions are transparent.

2. Add soup stock, increase heat to high, and bring to a boil. Boil for 5 minutes, then reduce heat to medium-low, and add cumin, paprika, and coriander. Season with salt and pepper; then cover and simmer for about 40 minutes, or until barley is tender.

3. Remove from heat and mash gently with a potato masher. Serve hot.

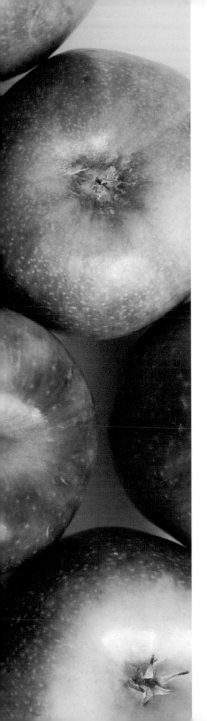

SALADS

GRILLED APPLE
AND CHICKEN SALAD

Great for entertaining, this salad tastes as good as it looks.

INGREDIENTS

Serves 4

5 tablespoons virgin olive oil, plus more for greasing

2 tablespoons cider vinegar

2 cloves garlic, crushed

3 tablespoons fresh rosemary needles, coarsely chopped

1 pound boneless and skinless chicken breast, thinly sliced

Salt and freshly ground black pepper

1 pound pumpkin or other winter squash, peeled and thinly sliced

3 unpeeled Red Delicious apples, cored and thinly sliced

10 ounces fresh asparagus, trimmed

½ cup apple juice

½ teaspoon soy sauce

½ pound arugula, trimmed

PREPARATION

1. Lightly grease a grill pan, and preheat over medium heat.

2. In a medium bowl, whisk together 4 tablespoons oil, vinegar, garlic, and rosemary until well combined.

3. Season chicken with salt and pepper. Transfer to bowl with oil mixture, and move chicken around until coated. Transfer chicken to grill pan using a slotted spoon and reserve oil mixture. Cook chicken for about 7 minutes on each side, or until golden on both sides and juices run clear. Transfer chicken to a large plate, and cover.

4. Place pumpkin, apples, and asparagus in reserved oil mixture and stir until coated. Transfer in batches to grill pan, and cook for 4 to 6 minutes on each side, or until tender. (Brush grill pan lightly with more oil if necessary.) Transfer to a large bowl, and cover.

5. In a small bowl, whisk together apple juice, soy sauce, and remaining tablespoon oil until well combined.

6. Add chicken and arugula to apple mixture, and toss gently to combine. Transfer to a large salad platter, and drizzle with apple juice mixture just before serving.

SPINACH, APPLE, AND WHEAT BERRY SALAD

Celebrate summer with this wholesome and colorful salad.

INGREDIENTS

Serves 4

2 cups salted water

½ cup wheat berries

7 ounces baby spinach leaves, trimmed

1 small red onion, thinly sliced

1 medium unpeeled Granny Smith apple, cored and thinly sliced

1 medium unpeeled Fuji apple, cored and thinly sliced

⅓ cup toasted walnuts

⅓ cup thickly sliced strawberries

2 tablespoons walnut or hazelnut oil

2 tablespoons raspberry vinegar

¾ cup cubed feta cheese

2 tablespoons chopped fresh parsley, for garnish

1 tablespoon chopped fresh basil, for garnish

PREPARATION

1. In a medium pot, bring water and wheat berries to a boil over high heat. Reduce heat to medium-low, cover, and simmer for 25 to 30 minutes, or until wheat berries are tender. Remove from heat, drain, and let cool, covered, for about 15 minutes.

2. In a medium bowl, mix together spinach, onion, apple, walnuts, strawberries, oil, vinegar, and cheese. Gently toss in wheat berries. Transfer to a salad plate and serve, garnished with parsley and basil.

QUINOA AND APPLE SALAD

This salad makes a light, healthy, and refreshing side dish. Great for serving in the summer with grilled fish, chicken, or meat.

INGREDIENTS

Serves 4 to 6

1 cup quinoa, rinsed and drained

2½ cups salted water

½ cup couscous

1 cup boiling vegetable or chicken stock

2 scallions, finely chopped

3 unpeeled Fuji apples, cored and thinly sliced

⅓ cup coarsely chopped toasted pecans

⅓ cup dried cranberries

2 tablespoons finely chopped cilantro

1 tablespoon finely chopped fresh mint

1 tablespoon finely chopped chives

2 tablespoons extra-virgin olive oil

1 teaspoon finely grated lemon rind

1 teaspoon finely grated orange rind

1 tablespoon lemon juice

1 tablespoon orange juice

Salt and freshly ground mixed peppercorns

PREPARATION

1. In a medium heavy-based saucepan, dry-roast quinoa over medium heat for 2 minutes. Add water, increase heat to high, and bring to a boil. Reduce heat to medium-low and simmer, covered, for about 20 minutes, or until water evaporates and quinoa is cooked through. Transfer to large bowl, fluff with a fork, and set aside.

2. Put couscous in a medium heatproof bowl. Pour in boiling soup stock, do not stir, and cover. Let sit for 15 minutes; then fluff with a fork, and stir into bowl with quinoa.

3. In a separate medium bowl, mix together scallions, apples, pecans, cranberries, cilantro, mint, chives, oil, rinds, and juices; season with salt and pepper. Transfer mixture to bowl with quinoa, and mix gently until well combined. Cover with plastic wrap, and refrigerate for at least 1 hour before serving to allow flavors to blend.

FRUIT AND NUT SALAD

With its combination of sweet and savory flavors, this salad is tasty and interesting, not to mention filling and satisfying. For best flavor, serve within an hour or two of preparation.

INGREDIENTS

Serves 4 to 6

2 tablespoons red wine vinegar

¼ cup mayonnaise

2 tablespoons grainy mustard

¼ cup honey

1 tablespoon warm water

¼ teaspoon salt

2 small unpeeled nectarines, pitted and thinly sliced

1 large mango, peeled, pitted, and thinly sliced

8 large strawberries, thinly sliced

1 large avocado, pitted, peeled, and thinly sliced

2 small unpeeled Fuji apples, cored and thinly sliced

2 small unpeeled Granny Smith apples, cored and thinly sliced

4 dried figs, thinly sliced

⅓ cup candied pecans halves

⅓ cup Brazil nut halves

⅓ cup toasted macadamia nut halves

5 ounces butter lettuce leaves

Handful sunflower seed sprouts, for garnish

PREPARATION

1. In a large bowl, whisk together vinegar, mayonnaise, mustard, honey, water, and salt until smooth and creamy.

2. Add nectarines, mango, strawberries, avocado, apples, figs, pecans, Brazil nuts, and macadamia nuts, and toss gently until coated.

3. Arrange lettuce on a salad platter and distribute fruit mixture evenly over top. Sprinkle with sprouts just before serving.

SMOKED SALMON AND APPLE SALAD

This salad makes a lovely and flavorful summertime supper.

INGREDIENTS

Serves 4

One 6-ounce bag mixed salad greens (such as baby spinach, arugula, and watercress)

½ pound boiled baby potatoes, thinly sliced

3½ ounces smoked salmon, thinly sliced

1 small red onion, thinly sliced

1 cup buttermilk

2 tablespoons mayonnaise

1 teaspoon plus 1 tablespoon lemon juice

1 teaspoon finely grated lemon rind

1 teaspoon sugar

Salt and freshly ground black pepper

1 large unpeeled Granny Smith apple, cored and thinly sliced

1 large unpeeled Fuji apple, cored and thinly sliced

PREPARATION

1. In a medium bowl, gently toss together salad greens, potatoes, salmon, and onion.

2. In a small bowl, whisk together buttermilk, mayonnaise, 1 teaspoon lemon juice, lemon rind, and sugar; season with salt and pepper. Transfer to a jar with a screw-top lid, and refrigerate until ready to serve.

3. In a medium bowl, toss together apples and remaining tablespoon lemon juice until apples are coated. Transfer to bowl with salad greens and toss gently. Transfer to a medium salad bowl, cover with plastic wrap, and refrigerate until ready to serve. Shake dressing vigorously just before serving, and serve on the side, or drizzle with dressing just before serving.

ROASTED APPLE AND BEET SALAD

This salad is fresh, sweet, and colorful—an attractive mealtime addition.

INGREDIENTS

Serves 4

4 small beets, trimmed and cut into quarters

4 small unpeeled Golden Delicious apples, cored and quartered

2 tablespoons extra-virgin olive oil

2 tablespoons apple juice

2 tablespoons lemon juice

2 tablespoons honey

Salt and freshly ground black pepper

4 ounces arugula

½ cup whole almonds

PREPARATION

1. Preheat oven to 325°F. Line 2 baking sheets with parchment paper.

2. Place beets on a baking sheet and brush with 1 tablespoon oil. Bake for 45 to 60 minutes, or until cooked through and crisp. Meanwhile, place apples on other baking sheet and brush with remaining tablespoon oil. Bake for 15 to 20 minutes, or until cooked through and crisp. Set aside beets and apples to cool.

3. In a small bowl, whisk together apple juice, lemon juice, and honey until well combined; season with salt and pepper.

4. Arrange arugula on a medium salad platter. Arrange apples and beets on top, drizzle with dressing, and sprinkle with almonds. Serve immediately.

SPICY APPLE, BRIE, AND RICE SALAD

This makes a light but substantial meal in a bowl, or a great accompaniment to grilled fish or steak.

INGREDIENTS

Serves 4

1½ cups short-grain brown rice

3 cups salted water

1 teaspoon butter

1 teaspoon canola oil

1 medium onion, thinly sliced

1 scallion, thinly sliced

3 strands saffron, soaked in 2 tablespoons boiling vegetable or chicken stock

2 celery stalks, thinly sliced

Salt and freshly ground black pepper

2 ounces Brie cheese, with rind and coarsely chopped

⅓ cup currants

4 ounces arugula, finely chopped

⅓ cup coarsely chopped toasted pecans

1 teaspoon finely chopped red chile

1 teaspoon light brown sugar

1 teaspoon lemon juice

1 tablespoon walnut or sesame oil

2 medium unpeeled Fuji apples, cored and finely chopped

PREPARATION

1. In a medium pot, bring rice and water to a boil over high heat. Reduce heat to medium-low, cover, and simmer for about 25 minutes, or until liquid has evaporated and rice is tender. Remove from heat and set aside, covered.

2. In a heavy-based medium saucepan, heat butter and oil over medium heat until butter melts. Add onion, scallion, saffron with stock, and celery, season with salt and pepper, and sauté for 6 to 8 minutes, until vegetables are tender and golden.

3. Fluff rice with a fork; then transfer to a medium salad bowl. Gently stir in onion mixture; then add cheese, currants, arugula, and pecans, tossing gently until well combined.

4. In a small bowl, whisk together chile, sugar, lemon juice, and oil until well combined. Add apples, and toss to coat.

5. Transfer apples and dressing to rice mixture, mixing gently to combine. Cover with plastic wrap and let sit at room temperature for at least 30 minutes before serving to allow flavors to blend.

THAI-STYLE GREEN APPLE SALAD

This refreshing salad is colorful, delicious, and healthy. Great for serving with beef or chicken.

INGREDIENTS

Serves 4

2 tablespoons sesame or peanut oil

4 scallions, cut into thin 2½-inch sticks

2 medium carrots, peeled and cut into thin 2½-inch sticks

2 celery stalks, cut into thin 2½-inch sticks

Salt

3 unpeeled Granny Smith apples, cored and thinly sliced

4 tablespoons lime juice

1 clove garlic, crushed

1 teaspoon finely chopped red chile

1 teaspoon sugar

1 tablespoon soy sauce

½ teaspoon ginger paste or minced fresh ginger

1 tablespoon finely chopped cilantro

16 cherry tomatoes, halved

1 cup bean sprouts

⅓ cup coarsely chopped roasted peanuts, for garnish

PREPARATION

1. In a medium heavy-based saucepan, heat oil over medium-high heat. Add scallions, carrots, celery, and salt, and sauté for 3 to 5 minutes, or until vegetables are just tender. Drain off oil, and set vegetables aside.

2. In a medium bowl, toss together apples and 2 tablespoons lime juice until apples are coated.

3. In a separate medium bowl, whisk together garlic, chile, sugar, soy sauce, remaining 2 tablespoons lime juice, ginger, and cilantro until well combined. Add tomatoes, bean sprouts, and carrot mixture, and toss gently until vegetables are coated.

4. Strain apples and arrange on a salad platter. Scatter vegetables with dressing over apples. Cover with plastic wrap and let sit at room temperature for at least 20 minutes before serving to allow flavors to blend. Garnish with peanuts just before serving.

APPLE, CHICKEN, AND WASABI SALAD

This tangy and refreshing salad has an Asian flair.

INGREDIENTS

Serves 4

4 cups salted water

1¾ pounds boneless and skinless chicken breast

1 teaspoon wasabi paste or powder

6 tablespoons mayonnaise

2 unpeeled Granny Smith apples, cored and thickly sliced

2 tablespoons lime juice

3 chives, finely chopped

1 small red onion, finely chopped

1 tablespoon black sesame seeds

PREPARATION

1. In a medium heavy-based saucepan, bring water to a boil over high heat. Add chicken, reduce heat to medium-low, cover, and poach for about 10 minutes, or until chicken is cooked through. Cool chicken in liquid for 10 minutes; then drain and shred into small pieces.

2. In a medium bowl, whisk together wasabi and mayonnaise until smooth. Add chicken and mix gently until chicken is coated.

3. In a medium salad bowl, toss together apples and lime juice until apples are coated. Mix in chives and red onion. Add chicken, and toss gently to combine. Sprinkle with sesame seeds and serve, or cover with plastic wrap and refrigerate until ready to serve.

BREADS, MUFFINS, AND COOKIES

APPLE AND PUMPKIN LOAF

This moist loaf has a lovely streusel topping. It makes an excellent addition to your picnic basket.

INGREDIENTS

Makes one 9 × 5-inch loaf

2½ cups all-purpose flour

2 cups light brown sugar

1 tablespoon ground nutmeg

1 teaspoon baking soda

½ teaspoon salt

2 large eggs

8 ounces canned pumpkin

2 small Golden Delicious apples, peeled, cored, and coarsely grated

½ cup canola oil

PREPARATION

1. Preheat oven to 350°F. Line a 9 × 5-inch loaf pan with parchment paper.

2. In a medium bowl, whisk together flour, sugar, nutmeg, baking soda, and salt until combined.

3. In a separate medium bowl, combine eggs, pumpkin, apples, and oil. Fold apple mixture into flour mixture until just combined. Pour batter into pan, and bake for 50 to 60 minutes, or until top is golden and a toothpick inserted in center of loaf comes out clean. Transfer pan to a wire rack and let stand 10 minutes; then turn loaf out onto rack and cool completely before slicing.

CHOCOLATE CHIP APPLE COOKIES

Here's a traditional cookie with a fruity twist.

INGREDIENTS

Makes 20 small cookies

½ cup butter, softened

½ teaspoon pure vanilla extract

⅓ cup superfine sugar

⅓ cup packed brown sugar

1 large egg

1 cup all-purpose flour

½ teaspoon baking soda

5 ounces milk chocolate, coarsely chopped

½ cup peeled, cored, and finely chopped Granny Smith apple

PREPARATION

1. Preheat oven to 350°F. Line 2 baking sheets with parchment paper.

2. In a medium bowl, beat butter, vanilla, sugars, and egg until smooth and creamy.

3. In a small bowl, sift together flour and baking soda. Fold flour mixture into butter mixture, stirring until combined. Mix in chocolate and apples.

4. Drop tablespoons of dough onto baking sheets, about 2 inches apart. Bake for 13 to 15 minutes, or until golden. Transfer sheets to wire racks and let cookies cool completely.

Opposite: Apple and Pumpkin Loaf

CRANBERRY-APPLE LOAF

This festive bread is lovely for serving at holidays or afternoon tea.

INGREDIENTS

Makes one 9 × 5-inch loaf

1 cup all-purpose flour

½ cup whole-wheat flour

1½ teaspoons baking powder

½ teaspoon baking soda

2 tablespoons finely grated orange rind

2 small Golden Delicious apples, peeled, cored, and finely chopped

¾ cup light brown sugar

2 tablespoons canola oil

1 large egg, lightly beaten

1 teaspoon pure vanilla extract

1 cup dried cranberries

½ cup coarsely chopped Brazil nuts

Butter for greasing

PREPARATION

1. Preheat oven to 350°F. Lightly grease a 9 × 5-inch loaf pan.

2. In a medium bowl, sift together flours, baking powder, and baking soda. Whisk in orange rind.

3. In a separate medium bowl, combine apples, sugar, and oil. Mix in egg and vanilla.

4. Fold flour mixture into apple mixture until just combined. Fold in cranberries and nuts. (Don't worry if it appears that you have too little batter.) Spoon batter into pan, and bake for 35 to 45 minutes, or until top is golden and a toothpick inserted in center of loaf comes out clean. Turn loaf out onto a wire rack, and cool completely before slicing.

APPLE AND SPICE MUFFINS

This wholesome treat is great for breakfast, or for a healthy snack between meals.

INGREDIENTS

Makes 12 muffins

Muffins:

1½ cups all-purpose flour

¾ cup muesli (blend of grains, nuts, and dried fruit)

¾ cup light brown sugar

½ teaspoon salt

2 teaspoons baking powder

½ teaspoon ground cinnamon

½ teaspoon ground nutmeg

½ teaspoon ground ginger

½ cup canola oil

1 large egg

⅓ cup milk

2 Golden Delicious apples, peeled, cored, and finely chopped

Butter for greasing

Topping:

1 teaspoon ground cinnamon

3 tablespoons light brown sugar

PREPARATION

1. Preheat oven to 375°F. Grease a 12-cup muffin pan.

2. Prepare muffins: In a medium bowl, combine flour, muesli, sugar, salt, baking powder, cinnamon, nutmeg, and ginger.

3. In a separate medium bowl, whisk together oil, egg, and milk. Fold in flour mixture until just combined. Fold in apples. Spoon batter into muffin cups, filling each cup ¾ full.

4. Prepare topping: In a small bowl, combine cinnamon and sugar. Sprinkle topping onto each muffin, and bake for 20 to 25 minutes, or until tops are golden and a toothpick inserted into center muffin comes out clean. Transfer pan to a wire rack and let stand 10 minutes. Turn muffins out onto rack to cool completely.

APPLE, LEMON, AND POPPY SEED MUFFINS WITH MINT SYRUP

Fresh mint syrup adds a refreshing touch to these lemony muffin.

INGREDIENTS

Makes 12 muffins

Muffins:

2 cups all-purpose flour

2 tablespoons poppy seeds

½ teaspoon salt

1¼ teaspoons baking powder

¼ teaspoon baking soda

½ cup unsalted butter, softened

¾ cup sugar

2 large eggs

1 tablespoon finely grated lemon rind

1 cup plain yogurt

1 teaspoon pure vanilla extract

1 large Granny Smith apple, peeled, cored, and finely chopped

Butter for greasing

Syrup:

1 cup superfine sugar

⅔ cup lemon juice

⅓ cup water

¼ cup firmly packed fresh mint leaves

PREPARATION

1. Preheat oven to 375°F. Grease a 12-cup muffin pan.

2. Prepare muffins: In a medium bowl, whisk together flour, poppy seeds, salt, baking powder, and baking soda.

3. In a separate medium bowl, beat butter and sugar until smooth and creamy. Beat in eggs, one at a time, beating well between additions. Add lemon rind, yogurt, and vanilla, beating until well combined.

4. Stir in flour mixture, mixing until just combined. Fold in apple. Spoon batter into muffin cups, filling each cup ¾ full. Bake for 20 to 25 minutes, or until tops are golden and a toothpick inserted into center muffin comes out clean.

5. In the meantime, prepare syrup: In a small saucepan, combine sugar, lemon juice, water, and mint leaves. Heat over medium-high heat while stirring for about 3 to 5 minutes, or until sugar dissolves. Do not boil. Reduce heat to medium-low, and simmer for about 2 minutes without stirring. Pour through a strainer into a heatproof pitcher.

6. When muffins are ready, transfer to a wire rack and let stand 10 minutes. Turn muffins out onto rack and position rack over a tray. Drizzle hot syrup over muffin tops, and let sit for at least 30 minutes, to allow muffins to absorb syrup.

APPLE AND DATE LOAF

Serve this delicious bread hot or cold. Great for afternoon tea or brunch.

INGREDIENTS

Makes one 9 × 5-inch loaf

¾ cup finely chopped pitted dates

⅓ cup boiling water

½ teaspoon baking soda

¼ cup pure maple syrup

½ cup butter, softened

⅓ cup packed dark brown sugar

2 large eggs

¾ cup self-rising whole-wheat flour

½ cup all-purpose flour

2 small Granny Smith apples, peeled, cored, and finely chopped

Butter for greasing

PREPARATION

1. Preheat oven to 350°F. Grease a 9 × 5-inch loaf pan.

2. In a small heatproof bowl, combine dates and boiling water. Stir in baking soda and let sit for 5 minutes. Stir in maple syrup.

3. In a separate medium bowl, beat butter and sugar until light and fluffy. Add eggs, one at a time, beating between additions until just combined.

4. Mix date mixture into butter mixture. In a small bowl sift flours together, then add in batches to butter mixture, mixing between each addition to combine. Fold in apples. Spoon batter into pan, and bake for about 50 minutes, or until top is golden and a toothpick inserted in center of loaf comes out clean. Transfer pan to a wire rack and let stand 10 minutes before turning loaf out onto rack.

ORANGE, APPLE, AND CRANBERRY MUFFINS

Need a break from yogurt and granola? This fruity muffin is great for breakfast, brunch, or afternoon tea.

INGREDIENTS

Makes 24 muffins

Muffins:

1 cup rolled oats

1 cup orange juice

1 teaspoon finely grated orange rind

1 cup canola oil

3 large eggs, beaten

3 cups all-purpose flour

1 cup light brown sugar

4 teaspoons baking powder

1 teaspoon salt

½ teaspoon baking soda

2 cups dried cranberries

1 large Golden Delicious apple, peeled, cored, and coarsely chopped

Butter for greasing

Topping:

½ cup chopped pecans

3 tablespoons light brown sugar

½ teaspoon ground cinnamon

PREPARATION

1. Preheat oven to 400°F. Grease two 12-cup muffin pans.

2. Prepare muffins: In a medium bowl, combine oats, orange juice, and orange rind. Mix in oil and eggs and set aside.

3. In a separate medium bowl, whisk together flour, sugar, baking powder, salt, and baking soda. Add cranberries.

4. Fold flour mixture into orange juice mixture until just combined. Fold in apple. Spoon batter into muffin cups, filling each cup ¾ full.

5. Prepare topping: In a small bowl, combine pecans, sugar, and cinnamon. Sprinkle topping onto each muffin; then bake muffins for 18 to 20 minutes, or until tops are golden and a toothpick inserted into center muffin comes out clean. Transfer pan to a wire rack and let stand 10 minutes; then turn muffins out onto rack to cool completely.

CARROT AND APPLE MUFFINS

This favorite muffin becomes a decadent dessert thanks to its sweet citrus topping.

INGREDIENTS

Makes 18 small muffins

Muffins:

½ cup coarsely chopped pecans or walnuts

1 cup all-purpose flour

1 cup whole-wheat flour

1¼ cups light brown sugar

½ teaspoon baking powder

¾ teaspoon baking soda

½ teaspoon salt

1 teaspoon ground cinnamon

½ teaspoon ground nutmeg

3 large eggs

¾ cup canola oil

1½ teaspoons pure vanilla extract

⅓ cup walnuts, chopped coarsely

2 medium carrots, peeled and grated

1 cup flaked coconut

2 medium Golden Delicious apples, peeled, cored, and finely chopped

Butter for greasing

Topping:

2 tablespoons orange juice

2 teaspoons finely grated orange rind

1 cup confectioners' sugar

PREPARATION

1. Preheat oven to 350°F. Grease an 18-cup muffin pan.

2. Prepare muffins: In a small, heavy-based pan, toast pecans over medium heat for about 8 minutes, or until fragrant. Set aside.

3. In a large bowl, whisk together flours, sugar, baking powder, baking soda, salt, cinnamon, and nutmeg.

4. In a separate large bowl, whisk together eggs, oil, and vanilla. Gently fold flour mixture into egg mixture. Fold in walnuts, carrots, coconut, and apples until just combined. Spoon batter into muffin cups, filling each cup ¾ full. Bake for 20 to 25 minutes, or until tops are golden and a toothpick inserted into center muffin comes out clean. Transfer pan to wire rack and let stand 10 minutes; then turn muffins out onto rack to cool completely.

5. Prepare topping: In a small bowl, combine orange juice, orange rind, and sugar. Mix until smooth, then drizzle onto cooled muffins.

APPLE BLONDIES

These blondies are a great variation on a classic theme; they include decadent white chocolate, fresh apples, and crunchy walnuts.

INGREDIENTS

Makes 16 brownies

½ cup butter, cut into pieces

10½ ounces white chocolate, chopped

½ cup superfine sugar

2 large eggs, lightly beaten

1¼ cups all-purpose flour

1 large Granny Smith apple, peeled, cored, and finely chopped

⅓ cup walnuts or macadamia nuts, coarsely chopped

PREPARATION

1. Preheat oven to 350°F. Line a deep 8 × 8-inch pan with parchment paper.

2. In a medium saucepan, heat butter and 7 ounces white chocolate over low heat, stirring constantly, until melted. Remove from heat and let sit for about 10 minutes to cool.

3. Stir in sugar and eggs, mixing until well combined. Add flour, remaining 3½ ounces white chocolate, apple, and nuts, stirring just until combined. Spread mixture into pan, and bake for about 35 minutes, or until firm to the touch. Cool completely in pan; then cut into 1-inch squares.

APPLE, DATE, AND GINGER MUFFINS

Start your day off right with this fiber-rich muffin.

INGREDIENTS

Makes 12 muffins

1 cup all-purpose flour

1 cup whole-wheat flour

⅔ cup light brown sugar, plus more for sprinkling

2 teaspoons baking powder

½ teaspoon baking soda

½ teaspoon salt

1 tablespoon ground ginger

½ teaspoon ground cinnamon

⅓ cup apple juice

⅔ cup buttermilk

1 large egg, lightly beaten

1 teaspoon pure vanilla extract

¼ cup unsalted butter, melted and cooled

⅔ cup finely chopped pitted dates

1 large Golden Delicious apple, peeled, cored, and finely chopped

PREPARATION

1. Preheat oven to 400°F. Grease a 12-cup muffin pan.

2. In a large bowl, whisk together flours, sugar, baking powder, baking soda, salt, ginger, and cinnamon.

3. In a separate medium bowl, whisk together apple juice, buttermilk, egg, vanilla, and butter.

4. Add buttermilk mixture to flour mixture, mixing until just combined. Fold in dates and apple. Spoon batter into muffin cups, filling each cup ¾ full. Sprinkle with sugar, and bake for 20 to 25 minutes, or until tops are golden and a toothpick inserted in center muffin comes out clean. Transfer pan to a wire rack and let stand 10 minutes; then turn muffins out onto rack and cool completely.

APPLE AND DATE SPICE COOKIES

These spicy cookies are great for giving as gifts during the festive season.

INGREDIENTS

Makes 30 small cookies

2 cups sifted all-purpose flour

1 teaspoon baking soda

½ teaspoon salt

1 teaspoon ground ginger

1 teaspoon ground nutmeg

½ teaspoon ground cloves

½ teaspoon ground white pepper

½ cup butter, softened

1⅓ cups packed dark brown sugar

⅓ cup apple juice

1 cup finely chopped almonds

1 cup finely chopped pitted dates

1 cup peeled, cored, and coarsely chopped Granny Smith apples

PREPARATION

1. Preheat oven to 400°F. Line 2 baking sheets with parchment paper.

2. In a medium bowl, whisk together flour, baking soda, salt, ginger, nutmeg, cloves, and white pepper.

3. In a large bowl, beat butter and sugar until smooth and creamy. Mix in apple juice until well combined. Fold in flour mixture and mix until batter is smooth and very thick. Stir in almonds, dates, and apples, mixing until well combined.

4. Drop tablespoons of dough onto baking sheet, about 2 inches apart. Bake for 10 to 12 minutes, or until golden and firm to the touch. Transfer sheets to wire racks and let cool for 5 minutes; then turn cookies out onto racks and cool completely.

APPLE OATMEAL COOKIES

This cookie is crispy on the outside and chewy on the inside; perfect for dunking in milk.

INGREDIENTS

Makes 20 large cookies

¾ cup butter

1 cup light brown sugar

1 large egg

1 teaspoon pure vanilla extract

¾ cup all-purpose flour

½ teaspoon baking soda

½ teaspoon salt

½ teaspoon ground nutmeg

3 cups rolled oats

1 cup coarsely chopped walnuts

2½ cups peeled, cored, and coarsely grated Granny Smith apples

PREPARATION

1. Preheat oven to 350°F. Line 2 baking sheets with parchment paper.

2. In a medium bowl, beat butter and sugar until smooth and creamy. Add egg and vanilla, and continue beating until smooth.

3. In a separate medium bowl, whisk together flour, baking soda, salt, and nutmeg. Add flour mixture to butter mixture, mixing until combined. Stir in oats, walnuts, and apples, and mix until combined.

4. Form 2–tablespoon balls of dough and place on baking sheet, leaving about 2 inches between each ball. Wet hands and gently press each cookie to flatten. Bake for 15 to 20 minutes, or until edges are golden but center is still slightly soft. Transfer sheets to wire racks and let stand for 5 minutes; then turn cookies out onto racks and cool completely.

CHOCOLATE-COATED APPLE CRANBERRY COOKIES

These cookies are soft, buttery, and very attractive.

INGREDIENTS

Makes 30 medium cookies

½ cup butter, softened

1½ cups packed dark brown sugar

1 large egg

¼ cup milk

2 tablespoons lemon juice

3 cups all-purpose flour

1 teaspoon baking powder

½ teaspoon salt

¼ teaspoon baking soda

1½ cups dried cranberries

1 cup peeled, cored, and finely chopped Granny Smith apples

3 ounces dark or white chocolate, chopped

PREPARATION

1. Preheat oven to 375°F. Line 2 baking sheets with parchment paper.

2. In a large bowl, beat butter and sugar until smooth and creamy. Add egg, milk, and lemon juice, beating until well combined.

3. In a separate large bowl, whisk together flour, baking powder, salt, and baking soda. Stir flour mixture into butter mixture and mix well. Add cranberries and apples, mixing until combined.

4. Drop tablespoons of dough onto baking sheets, about 2 inches apart. Bake for 13 to 15 minutes, or until golden. Transfer sheets to wire racks and let stand for 5 minutes; then turn cookies out onto racks and cool completely.

5. When cookies have cooled, melt chocolate in top of double boiler. Remove chocolate from heat; then dip each cookie halfway into chocolate. Arrange cookies on parchment paper and let sit until chocolate hardens. To store, line an airtight container with parchment paper, and lay cookies flat. Place a piece of parchment paper between each layer of cookies.

APPLE MUESLI COOKIES

Brimming with fruit and nuts, this cookie makes a healthy midday snack or a tasty breakfast treat.

INGREDIENTS

Makes 20 medium cookies

1 cup muesli (blend of grains, nuts, and dried fruit)

1 cup all-purpose flour

1 cup superfine sugar

2 tablespoons ground cinnamon

¼ cup dried cranberries

⅓ cup finely chopped dried apricots

½ cup finely chopped almonds

½ cup butter

2 tablespoons honey

½ teaspoon baking soda

1 tablespoon boiling water

2 small Granny Smith apples, peeled, cored, and finely chopped

PREPARATION

1. Preheat oven to 300°F. Line 2 baking sheets with parchment paper.

2. In a large bowl, combine muesli, flour, sugar, cinnamon, cranberries, apricots, and almonds.

3. In a small saucepan, melt butter and honey over low heat.

4. In a small heatproof bowl, combine baking soda and boiling water. Add soda mixture to butter mixture and stir; then add butter mixture to dry ingredients, mixing until well combined. Fold in apples.

5. Shape dough into 1-inch balls and arrange on sheets, about 2 inches apart. Wet hands and gently press each cookie to flatten. Bake for about 20 minutes, or until edges are golden and center is still slightly soft. Transfer sheets to wire racks and let cookies cool completely.

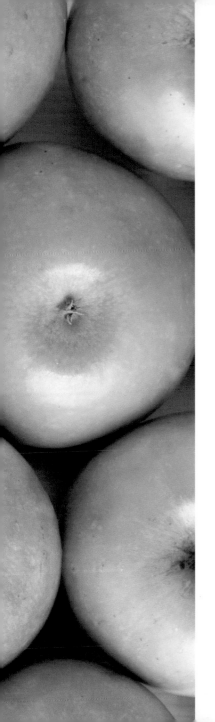

CHICKEN AND MEAT

ROASTED CHICKEN WITH CARAMELIZED FENNEL AND APPLES

This dish features a mouthwatering combination of fennel, roast chicken, and fruit. Excellent with roasted or baked potatoes.

INGREDIENTS

Serves 4

Chicken:

2 tablespoons olive oil

1 tablespoon lemon juice

8 drumsticks, with skin

2 tablespoons fennel seeds

Salt and freshly ground black pepper

Sauce:

¼ cup butter

2 teaspoons sugar

4 medium fennel heads, trimmed and thickly sliced lengthwise

3 unpeeled Fuji apples, cored and quartered

1 cup apple juice

¼ cup cider vinegar

¼ teaspoon salt

PREPARATION

1. Preheat oven to 400°F.

2. Prepare chicken: In a medium ovenproof casserole dish, mix together oil and lemon juice. Add drumsticks and move around to coat. Sprinkle with fennel seeds, season with salt and pepper, and bake, uncovered, for 40 minutes, or until chicken is golden and juices run clear.

3. Prepare sauce: In the meantime, in a large heavy-based saucepan, heat butter and sugar while stirring over medium-low heat, until mixture foams and sugar dissolves. Add fennel and apples, increase heat to medium-high, and cook for about 5 minutes, or until slightly golden.

4. Add apple juice, vinegar, and salt. Reduce heat to medium-low and simmer, covered, for about 15 minutes, or until apples and fennel are just tender.

5. Remove chicken from oven, and distribute apple mixture evenly over and between drumsticks. Increase heat to 450°F, and bake for 10 to 15 minutes, or until brown and crisp.

CITRUS GINGER CHICKEN

This dish is simple to make, delicious, and healthy. Serve with rice or couscous and steamed green beans.

INGREDIENTS

Serves 4

½ cup orange juice

½ cup lemon or lime juice

2 tablespoons honey

1 tablespoon ginger paste or minced fresh ginger

2 bay leaves

4 boneless and skinless chicken breasts

Salt and freshly ground black pepper

1 tablespoon butter

1 medium orange, peeled, split into segments, and seeded

1 medium Fuji apple, peeled and thickly sliced

1 small lemon, thickly sliced

Vegetable oil for greasing

PREPARATION

1. In a medium bowl, whisk together juices, honey, and ginger. Add the bay leaves.

2. Season chicken with salt and pepper. Grease a nonstick heavy-based skillet, and heat over medium-high heat. Cook chicken for 2 minutes on each side, or until slightly golden.

3. Pour orange juice mixture into pan and stir. Increase heat to high and bring to a boil. Immediately reduce heat to medium-low and simmer, covered, for 8 to 10 minutes, or until chicken is cooked through and white when pierced.

4. Transfer chicken to a serving dish using a slotted spoon, and heat sauce in pan to boiling. Add butter, orange, apple, and lemon. Reduce heat to medium-low and cook while stirring gently until butter melts and sauce thickens slightly. Pour sauce over chicken, and serve immediately.

CHICKEN AND APPLE TAGINE

A simple dish that is excellent for serving with rice for a nutritious midweek meal.

INGREDIENTS

Serves 4

2 tablespoons olive oil

8 small boneless and skinless chicken thighs

1 medium red onion, coarsely chopped

2 teaspoons ginger paste or minced fresh ginger

½ cup chicken or vegetable stock

⅛ teaspoon saffron or turmeric

1 tablespoon honey

1 pound carrots, peeled and cut into 2-inch sticks

2 medium Granny Smith apples, peeled, cored, and thinly sliced

Salt and freshly ground black pepper

2 tablespoons roughly chopped parsley or cilantro, for garnish

Lemon wedges, for garnish

PREPARATION

1. In a large heavy-based saucepan, heat oil over medium heat. Add chicken and cook for about 3 minutes on each side, or until slightly golden. Stir in onion and ginger, and cook for 2 minutes.

2. Stir in soup stock, saffron, honey, carrots, and apples; season with salt and pepper. Increase heat to high and bring to a boil. Cover, then reduce heat to medium-low and simmer for 20 minutes, or until carrots and apples are tender.

3. Remove cover, increase heat to medium, and cook for about 5 minutes, to reduce sauce a bit. Garnish with parsley and lemon wedges before serving.

LEMON, APPLE, AND SAGE GRILLED CHICKEN

This classic combination is low in fat, tasty, and simple to prepare. Serve with spicy roasted potatoes.

INGREDIENTS

Serves 2

3 Granny Smith apples, peeled, cored, and coarsely chopped

2 tablespoons lemon juice

1 teaspoon light brown sugar

10 fresh sage leaves

Salt and freshly ground black pepper

2 boneless and skinless chicken breasts

1 tablespoon finely grated lemon rind

Olive oil for greasing

PREPARATION

1. In a small heavy-based saucepan, heat apples and lemon juice over medium heat. Add sugar and 5 sage leaves, and season with salt and pepper. Increase heat to high and bring to a boil while stirring. Immediately reduce heat to medium-low, cover, and simmer for about 6 minutes, or until apples are just tender. Remove from heat, and transfer to serving dish.

2. Heat grill pan to medium-high and brush with oil. Rub chicken with salt, pepper, and lemon rind, and sprinkle with remaining sage leaves. Cook for about 5 minutes on each side, or until chicken is golden with grill marks, and meat is tender and white when cut. Remove from grill pan, arrange on top of apples, and serve.

BEEF AND APPLE STIR-FRY

Adding apples to a traditional stir-fry imbues it with great flavor and sweetness.

INGREDIENTS

Serves 4

1 cup jasmine rice

2 cups salted water

1½ pounds beef rump steak, cut into thin 1-inch slices

1 clove garlic, crushed

2 tablespoons sweet chili sauce

1 tablespoon peanut or canola oil

2 tablespoons light soy sauce

1 medium yellow pepper, thinly sliced

1 medium zucchini, thinly sliced

½ pound green beans, halved

1 medium unpeeled Granny Smith apple, cored and thinly sliced

2 scallions, thinly sliced horizontally, plus more for garnish

½ cup toasted cashews

Salt and freshly ground black pepper

PREPARATION

1. In a medium saucepan, bring rice and water to a boil over high heat; immediately reduce heat to low and cook, covered, for about 20 minutes, or until water evaporates. Leave covered and set aside.

2. In a large bowl, mix together beef, garlic, and chili sauce. In a wok or large skillet, heat oil over medium-high heat; add beef in batches and stir-fry for 2 to 3 minutes, or until browned all over.

3. Add soy sauce, yellow pepper, zucchini, beans, apple, and scallions, and stir-fry for about 8 minutes, or until vegetables are tender and beef is cooked through. Add rice and cashews, season with salt and pepper, and stir-fry for about 2 minutes. Serve immediately, garnished with scallions.

APPLE AND SAGE BURGERS WITH CARAMELIZED ONIONS

For a burger with a savory twist, try this recipe. Serve with caramelized onions and fresh buns.

INGREDIENTS

Serves 4

2 pounds ground beef

1 medium red onion, finely chopped

1 medium Granny Smith apple, peeled, cored, and finely grated

1 large egg

2 tablespoons finely chopped fresh sage

Salt and freshly ground black pepper

Canola oil for frying

PREPARATION

1. In a large bowl, mix together beef, onion, apple, egg, and sage; season with salt and pepper. Wet hands and shape mixture into four patties.

2. In a large nonstick skillet, heat oil over medium heat. Fry patties in batches for 6 to 7 minutes on each side, or until cooked through.

FRUITY MEATBALL CASSEROLE

With few ingredients and a short cooking time, this dish is surprisingly easy to prepare. Serve with mashed or roasted potatoes.

INGREDIENTS

Serves 4

2 tablespoons canola oil

½ pound prepared meatballs, fresh or frozen and thawed

1 small onion, thinly sliced

3 tablespoons marmalade or chutney, any flavor

1¼ cups vegetable or beef stock

2 Fuji apples, peeled, cored, and thickly sliced

1 cup dried apricots

PREPARATION

1. In a large heavy-based saucepan, heat oil over medium-high heat. Add meatballs and onion, and cook for 2 minutes or until evenly browned.

2. Stir in marmalade, soup stock, apples, and apricots; increase heat to high, and bring to a boil. Reduce heat to medium-low and simmer, covered, for about 20 minutes, or until meatballs are cooked through and sauce has thickened. Serve immediately.

CRANBERRY-APPLE CHICKEN

*This dish is simple to prepare, healthy, and low in fat. Great for entertaining—
serve with mashed potatoes or parsnips and steamed green beans.*

INGREDIENTS

Serves 4

2 tablespoons olive oil

4 boneless and skinless
chicken breasts

Salt and freshly ground black
pepper

¼ cup cranberry sauce

1 large Granny Smith apple,
peeled, cored, and coarsely
chopped

1 tablespoon finely grated
orange rind

2 tablespoons orange juice

PREPARATION

1. In a large nonstick skillet,
heat oil over medium heat.
Season chicken with salt and
pepper; then cook for 3
minutes on each side, or until
lightly golden. Remove chicken
from pan and set aside.

2. In a large heavy-based
saucepan, heat cranberry
sauce, apple, and orange rind
over medium-low heat,
stirring occasionally, for about
10 minutes, or until apples are
just tender.

3. Stir in orange juice; then add
chicken, cover, and simmer
over medium-low heat until
chicken is white and tender.

APPLE AND SPICE CHICKEN

This festive sweet and spicy dish is lovely with steamed rice and baked winter squash.

INGREDIENTS

Serves 4

2 tablespoons canola oil

4 chicken thighs, with skin

Coarse salt

2 tablespoons butter

3 medium Granny Smith apples, peeled, cored, and thinly sliced

1 tablespoon lemon juice

1 tablespoon light brown sugar

½ cup apple juice

½ cup orange juice

2 tablespoons pure maple syrup or honey

1 teaspoon ginger paste or minced fresh ginger

3 whole nutmegs

4 small cinnamon sticks

5 star anise

PREPARATION

1. Preheat oven to 400°F.

2. Coat an ovenproof casserole dish with oil. Add chicken, sprinkle with salt, and bake for about 40 minutes, or until chicken is browned and juices run clear. Remove from oven and set aside.

3. In a medium heavy-based saucepan, heat butter over medium heat until melted. In a medium bowl, toss together apples and lemon juice until apples are coated; then add to saucepan. Stir in sugar and cook for about 5 minutes, or until apples are tender and just starting to brown. Remove from heat and set aside.

4. In a small bowl, mix together apple juice, orange juice, maple syrup, and ginger; then pour over chicken. Scatter nutmeg, cinnamon, star anise, and apples over and between chicken pieces. Increase heat to 450°F, and cook for 10 to 15 minutes, or until brown and crisp.

74

LAMB CHOPS WITH CARAMELIZED APPLES, ONIONS, AND MINT

Mint and apples are a perfect complement to the richness of the lamb chops in this dish.

INGREDIENTS

Serves 2

2 teaspoons butter

2 medium unpeeled Fuji apples, cored and thinly sliced

1 teaspoon sugar

1 tablespoon canola oil

2 lamb chops

1 small onion, thinly sliced

½ cup apple juice

2 tablespoons chopped fresh mint leaves, plus whole leaves for garnish

PREPARATION

1. In a small nonstick skillet, melt 1 teaspoon butter over medium heat. Add apples, sprinkle with sugar, and cook for about 3 minutes on each side, until golden. Remove from heat and set aside.

2. In a medium nonstick skillet, heat oil over medium heat. Add lamb chops and cook for about 3 minutes on each side, or until medium-rare. Transfer to a plate using a slotted spoon, and set aside.

3. In same pan, heat remaining teaspoon butter over medium-low heat until melted. Add onion and apple juice, and cook for about 4 minutes, or until onion is tender.

4. Return lamb chops to pan, add mint, and simmer for about 4 minutes, or until sauce has reduced and meat is tender. Transfer lamb chops to a serving dish, and arrange apples on the side. Garnish with mint and serve.

EASY BEEF AND APPLE CURRY

For a quick Thai-style curry, try this dish. Serve over basmati rice.

INGREDIENTS

Serves 2

1 tablespoon peanut or sesame oil

¾ pound lean sirloin steak, sliced into thin strips

2 tablespoons Thai curry paste

¼ cup water

1 teaspoon sugar

⅓ pound fine green beans, halved

1 large Granny Smith apple, peeled, cored, and thinly sliced

1 small red pepper, cored, seeded, and thinly sliced

Salt

2 tablespoons coarsely chopped roasted peanuts, for garnish

PREPARATION

1. In a large wok or heavy-based skillet, heat oil over high heat until smoking hot. Add steak and cook for about 2 minutes, or until browned all over.

2. Reduce heat to medium and stir in curry paste. Stir in water and sugar; then add beans, apple, red pepper, and salt to taste. Cook for 6 to 8 minutes, or until apples and vegetables are just tender. Add more water for more sauce if desired. Garnish with peanuts just before serving.

BRAISED BEEF WITH RED WINE, CRANBERRIES, AND APPLES

Enjoy the comforting aromas of cranberries, apples, and beef as this dish cooks.
Serve with creamy mashed potatoes.

INGREDIENTS

Serves 4

2 pounds beef sirloin steak, cut into 2-inch slices

Salt and freshly ground black pepper

2 to 3 tablespoons olive oil

3 small onions, peeled and thinly sliced

1¼ cups red wine

1¼ cups beef or vegetable stock

2 medium Granny Smith apples, peeled, cored, and coarsely chopped

3 heaping tablespoons cranberry sauce

Small bunch flat-leaf parsley, coarsely chopped

PREPARATION

1. Season meat with salt and pepper. In a large heavy-based saucepan, heat 2 tablespoons oil over medium-high heat; add meat in batches, and cook for 2 to 3 minutes on each side, or until browned all over. Transfer to a plate using a slotted spoon and set aside.

2. In same pan, heat remaining tablespoon oil (if necessary); add onions and cook over medium-high heat for about 5 minutes, or until slightly browned.

3. Return beef to pan, and add wine, soup stock, and apples; season with salt and pepper. Increase heat to high and bring to a boil, stirring regularly.

4. Reduce heat to medium-low, cover, and simmer for about 1½ hours, or until beef is very tender. Add cranberry sauce, and season again with salt and pepper. Simmer for 5 minutes, covered. Scatter parsley over top before serving.

79

POT ROAST WITH GLAZED APPLE AND PEARS

This slow-cooked dish fills the house with a delicious aroma as it cooks. Serve with plain rice or roasted potatoes.

INGREDIENTS

Serves 6

Roast:

One 3-pound beef chuck roast

2 teaspoons coriander seeds, crushed

4 bay leaves

4 cups beef or vegetable stock

1¼ cups red wine

Salt and freshly ground black pepper

Glazed fruit:

1 tablespoon lemon juice

4 small Granny Smith apples, peeled and with stem

4 small pears, peeled and with stem

4 cups water

1 teaspoon canola oil

¼ cup butter, melted

8 shallots, peeled

2 small cinnamon sticks

3 star anise

4 cardamom pods, bruised

3 whole allspice berries

6 tablespoons pure maple syrup or honey

PREPARATION

1. Prepare roast: Put beef in a large heavy pot, and sprinkle coriander and bay leaves over top. Pour in soup stock and wine, and season with salt and pepper. Cover and bring to a boil over high heat. Immediately reduce heat to low, and cook for 2 to 2½ hours, or until meat is cooked through and tender. Set aside to cool; then remove extra fat.

2. Prepare glazed fruit: In a large bowl, toss together lemon juice, apples, and pears until fruit is coated.

3. In a medium saucepan, bring water to a boil over high heat. Add apples and pears, reduce heat to medium-low, cover, and poach for about 30 minutes, or until fruit is tender.

4. In the meantime, preheat oven to 375°F. Place oil and butter in a small roasting dish. Transfer poached fruit using a slotted spoon, and add shallots, cinnamon, star anise, cardamom, and allspice. Brush fruit with maple syrup, and roast for about 1 hour, or until golden and soft. Turn fruit over occasionally during roasting, brushing twice with maple syrup.

5. To serve, spoon apples, pears, and sauce over beef, and reheat.

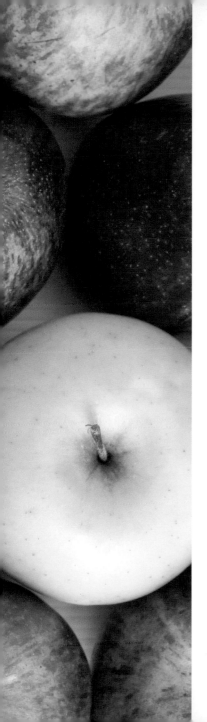

BEVERAGES
AND
CONDIMENTS

APPLE CHAMPAGNE

Treat your guests to an exotic non-alcoholic drink before dinner. (For an alcoholic twist, add a drop of gin.)

INGREDIENTS

Makes 13 cups

¾ cup freshly squeezed lemon juice (about 6 medium lemons)

⅓ cup superfine sugar

8 cups apple juice, chilled

4 cups sparkling water, chilled

2 small unpeeled Fuji apples, cored and thinly sliced

Handful fresh mint leaves, coarsely chopped

PREPARATION

1. In a small saucepan, heat lemon juice and sugar over low heat for about 8 minutes, or until a syrup forms. Set aside to cool.

2. In a large bowl, combine apple juice, sparkling water, and lemon syrup. Mix in apples and mint. Pour into champagne-style glasses and serve.

WARM APPLE WINE

A glass of this tangy punch is a great way to greet guests and lighten the mood.

INGREDIENTS

Makes 6 cups

½ cup light brown sugar

½ cup orange juice

1¼ cups apple juice

1 medium orange, halved, pitted, and thickly sliced

4 small cinnamon sticks

4 whole nutmegs

One 25-ounce bottle semi-sweet red wine

2 large unpeeled Granny Smith apples, cored, quartered, and thickly sliced

PREPARATION

1. In a medium pot, mix together sugar, juices, orange, cinnamon, and nutmeg. Bring to a boil over medium-high heat; then reduce heat to medium-low, cover, and simmer for 10 minutes.

2. Add wine and apples, and simmer for 10 minutes. Serve hot, in heatproof cups or glasses.

Opposite: Apple Champagne

FRUITY HOT CIDER

There's nothing like a cup of hot cider for warming up on a chilly day. This cider has a twist, thanks to its inclusion of cranberry juice, orange juice, star anise, and nutmeg.

INGREDIENTS

Makes 10 cups

4 cups apple juice

2 cups cranberry juice

2 cups orange juice

1½ cups apple cider

2 large bay leaves

3 star anise

2 medium cinnamon sticks

2 whole nutmegs

½ cup pure maple syrup

PREPARATION

1. In a large saucepan, mix together juices, cider, bay leaves, star anise, cinnamon, nutmeg, and maple syrup. Bring to a boil over high heat, and let boil, uncovered, for 5 minutes.

2. Reduce heat to medium-low and simmer for about 8 minutes, or until fragrant. Discard bay leaves, star anise, and nutmeg. Remove cinnamon sticks and use as garnish. Serve hot, in heatproof cups or glasses.

Opposite: Fruity Hot Cider

APPLE SALSA

This fresh salsa has an Asian flair, and makes a great appetizer. Serve with fresh bread or crispy corn chips.

INGREDIENTS

Serves 6

2 unpeeled Granny Smith apples, cored and finely chopped

¼ cup lime juice

1 tablespoon peanut oil

1 small fresh green chile, seeded and finely chopped

½ cup finely chopped red pepper

1 scallion, finely chopped

½ small red onion, finely chopped

2 tablespoons finely chopped fresh cilantro

2 tablespoons finely chopped peeled fresh ginger

½ cup chopped walnuts or cashews

Salt

PREPARATION

In a medium bowl, toss together apples and lime juice until apples are coated. Add peanut oil, chile, scallion, onion, cilantro, ginger, walnuts, and salt to taste. Mix until well combined; then cover and refrigerate for about 30 minutes before serving.

MANGO-APPLE CHUTNEY

You won't want your turkey or chicken leftovers to run out while this is still in your fridge. This chutney makes a delicious homemade gift as well.

INGREDIENTS

Makes 8 cups

2 tablespoons canola oil

2 onions, halved and thinly sliced

2 tablespoons thinly sliced peeled fresh ginger

½ teaspoon ground cardamom

2 small cinnamon sticks

1 teaspoon crushed cumin seeds

1 teaspoon crushed coriander seeds

1 teaspoon nigella seeds

¼ teaspoon ground turmeric

1 pound Granny Smith apples, peeled, cored, and coarsely chopped

2 cups water

4 pounds ripe mangos, peeled, pitted, and coarsely chopped

1 small red chile, seeded and finely chopped

1¼ cups cider vinegar

4 cups sugar

1 teaspoon salt

PREPARATION

1. In a large heavy-based saucepan, heat oil over medium heat. Add onions and sauté for about 3 minutes, or until onions begin to soften. Stir in ginger, cardamom, cinnamon, cumin, coriander, and nigella, and cook for 8 to 10 minutes, or until onions are golden and spices are fragrant.

2. Stir in turmeric, apples, and water. Increase heat to high, and bring mixture to a boil. Reduce heat to medium-low and cook, covered, for 10 minutes. Stir in mangos and chile, and cook for 20 minutes, or until apples are pulpy and mango is tender.

3. Add vinegar, sugar, and salt, and simmer, uncovered, for about 30 minutes, stirring frequently, until mixture is pulpy and not watery. Remove from heat and let cool completely; then spoon into airtight glass containers and refrigerate until ready to serve. May be stored in refrigerator for up to 6 months.

APRICOT, APPLE, AND PECAN STUFFING

Transform ordinary stuffing into decorative (and delicious) balls with this recipe. A perfect vegetarian alternative, as it isn't baked in a turkey.

INGREDIENTS

Makes 32 small balls

¼ cup butter

2 large onions, finely chopped

½ cup pecans, roughly chopped

2 medium Granny Smith apples, peeled, cored, and coarsely grated

½ cup dried apricots, finely chopped

1½ cups fresh breadcrumbs

¼ cup finely chopped fresh parsley

1 tablespoon finely grated lemon rind

1 large egg, beaten

Salt and freshly ground black pepper

Butter for greasing

Olive oil for drizzling

PREPARATION

1. Preheat oven to 350°F. Grease an 8 × 8-inch baking pan with butter.

2. In a medium heavy-based saucepan, heat butter over medium heat until melted. Add onions and sauté for about 3 minutes, or until onions are transparent. Stir in pecans and cook for about 5 minutes, or until onion is golden. Remove from heat.

3. Squeeze out excess liquid from apples, then add to onion mixture. Mix in apricots, breadcrumbs, parsley, and lemon rind. Stir in egg, and season with salt and pepper.

4. Wet hands and shape mixture into small balls. Arrange balls in baking dish, drizzle with oil, and bake for 30 minutes, or until golden and crisp.

APPLE BUTTER

This highly concentrated form of applesauce has a longer shelf life than regular applesauce due to its high sugar content. Spread it on buttered toast or fresh muffins, or serve as a sweet side dish.

INGREDIENTS

Makes 2 cups

2 cups applesauce

4 cups sugar

½ teaspoon ground cinnamon

⅛ teaspoon ground cloves

¼ cup water

PREPARATION

1. In a small pot, mix together applesauce, sugar, cinnamon, and cloves. Cover and cook over very low heat, stirring occasionally with a whisk, for 4 hours.

2. Add water and cook, uncovered, for 2 hours, or until sauce is reddish and quite thick. Remove from heat and let cool completely; then spoon into an airtight glass container and refrigerate until ready to serve. May be stored in refrigerator for up to 4 months.

APPLE, PINEAPPLE, GINGER, AND MINT SMOOTHIE

This light drink is sweet and spicy; a perfect refreshment for a hot summer day.

INGREDIENTS

Serves 2

1 cup peeled, cored and finely chopped apples, any variety

½ cup finely chopped pineapple

1 teaspoon ginger paste or minced fresh ginger

3 cups mint tea, cooled

4 ice cubes

PREPARATION

Place apples, pineapple, ginger, tea, and ice cubes in a blender and blend until smooth. Serve immediately.

Opposite: Apple Butter

APPLE CIDER DRESSING

This is a great dressing for serving with salad greens, steamed vegetables, or grilled chicken.

INGREDIENTS

Makes ½ cup

¼ cup apple cider vinegar

2 tablespoons olive oil

1 tablespoon grainy mustard

1 tablespoon honey

PREPARATION

In a jar with a screw-top lid, combine vinegar, oil, mustard, and honey. Close jar tightly and shake vigorously to combine. May be stored in refrigerator for up to 1 month.

APPLE, LEMON, AND YOGURT SMOOTHIE

Treat yourself with this creamy drink at mid-morning.

INGREDIENTS

Serves 2

1 cup peeled, cored, and finely chopped apples, any variety

3 cups lemon-flavored frozen yogurt

½ cup apple juice

PREPARATION

Place apples, yogurt, and apple juice in a blender, and blend until smooth. Serve immediately.

Opposite: Apple Cider Dressing

APPLESAUCE

Conjure memories of childhood with this traditional recipe. Great on its own, it's also delicious alongside ice cream, crumpets, rice pudding, meat, chicken, or turkey.

INGREDIENTS

Makes 2 cups

6 Fuji apples, peeled, cored, and quartered

2 tablespoons lemon juice

1 cup unfiltered apple juice

2 tablespoons butter

3 tablespoons honey

¼ teaspoon ground cinnamon

PREPARATION

1. In a medium saucepan, mix together apples, lemon juice, apple juice, butter, honey, and cinnamon. Cover and cook over medium heat for 15 to 20 minutes, or until apples are soft.

2. Mash with a potato masher to desired consistency. Serve warm or chilled. May be stored in refrigerator for up to 2 weeks.

SIMPLE APPLE AND DATE SPREAD

This is a lovely alternative to jam. Quick and easy to prepare, too!

INGREDIENTS

Makes 1 cup

1 cup pitted dates

1 cup apple juice

PREPARATION

1. In a small pot over medium-high heat, bring dates and apple juice to a boil. Reduce heat to medium-low and simmer, uncovered, stirring frequently, for about 8 minutes, or until apple juice is absorbed.

2. Remove from heat and let cool completely; then transfer to an airtight glass container, and refrigerate before serving. May be stored in refrigerator for up to 2 weeks.

APPLE CIDER SAUCE

This sauce is great for enriching meat, chicken, mashed potatoes, or rice.

INGREDIENTS

Makes 2 cups

1 cup sugar

1 tablespoon ground cinnamon

2 cups fresh apple cider

¼ cup lemon juice

¼ cup butter

PREPARATION

1. In a medium heavy-based saucepan, whisk together sugar and cinnamon. Add cider and lemon juice, and bring to a boil over high heat.

2. Reduce heat to medium-low and cook, uncovered, for 10 to 15 minutes, or until liquid reduces and sauce thickens. Stir in butter and remove from heat. Serve immediately or reheat just before serving.

APPLE RELISH

This unusual condiment is lovely alongside chicken, turkey, or beef.

INGREDIENTS

Makes 2 cups

4 Granny Smith apples, peeled, cored, and coarsely chopped

5 tablespoons light brown sugar

1 small cinnamon stick

½ teaspoon crushed dried chiles

¼ teaspoon ground nutmeg

½ cup apple cider

PREPARATION

1. In a small heavy-based saucepan, mix together apples, sugar, cinnamon, chiles, nutmeg, and cider. Cook over low heat for about 20 minutes, or until mixture reduces to a thick pulp.

2. Remove from heat and let cool completely; then transfer to an airtight glass container, and refrigerate before serving. May be stored in refrigerator for up to 1 week.

CLASSIC
APPLE CHUTNEY

This chutney features a wonderful combination of sweet and tart flavors. It's great for serving with chicken, meat, or vegetables, and is perfect for perking up cheeses.

INGREDIENTS

Makes 4 cups

1 pound Golden Delicious apples, peeled, cored, and coarsely chopped

1 large onion, finely chopped

1½ cups light brown sugar

½ cup white wine vinegar

¾ teaspoon freshly ground black pepper

2 tablespoons thinly sliced crystallized ginger

3 tablespoons seedless raisins

3 medium cinnamon sticks

3 small bay leaves

¼ teaspoon salt

PREPARATION

1. In a medium saucepan, combine apples, onion, sugar, vinegar, pepper, ginger, raisins, cinnamon, bay leaves, and salt. Cook over medium heat for about 8 minutes, stirring occasionally, until sugar dissolves.

2. Reduce heat to medium-low and simmer for about 45 minutes, or until mixture is syrupy and apples are soft. (Don't worry if mixture seems a little runny, as it will thicken as it cools.) Remove from heat and let cool completely; then spoon into airtight glass containers and refrigerate before serving. May be stored in refrigerator for up to 6 months.

APPLE MARMALADE

This versatile condiment goes with just about everything; spread on whole-grain bread, buttery croissants, or fresh scones, or use as a glaze for chicken, meat, or turkey dishes.

INGREDIENTS

Makes 4 cups

1½ cups apple juice

2½ cups sugar

8 small Granny Smith apples, peeled, cored, and finely chopped

½ large orange, sliced into thin small pieces and seeds removed

1 tablespoon lemon juice

PREPARATION

1. In a medium pot, bring apple juice and sugar to a boil over medium-high heat. Reduce heat to medium, and add apples, orange, and lemon juice. Cook, covered, for about 15 minutes, or until apples and oranges are tender.

2. Remove cover, reduce heat to medium-low, and simmer for about 20 minutes, or until mixture has reduced and thickened, and fruit has a jam-like consistency. Remove from heat and let cool completely; then spoon into airtight glass containers and refrigerate until ready to serve. May be stored in refrigerator for up to 3 months.

MUSHROOM, SAGE, AND APPLE STUFFING

Give this aromatic stuffing a try the next time you roast chicken. It's perfect for entertaining.

INGREDIENTS

Serves 6

1 tablespoon olive oil

2 tablespoons butter

1 large onion, coarsely grated

2 cups finely chopped button mushrooms

Salt and freshly ground black pepper

1 large Granny Smith apple, peeled, cored, and coarsely grated

2 tablespoons finely chopped fresh sage

1¼ cups fresh breadcrumbs

1 large egg, beaten

PREPARATION

1. In a medium heavy-based saucepan, heat oil and butter over medium heat until butter melts. Add onion and sauté for 3 minutes, or until onion is transparent.

2. Stir in mushrooms, increase heat to high, and cook for about 3 minutes. Season with salt and pepper; mix in apple and cook for 3 to 5 minutes, or until onions are golden.

3. Remove from heat, and stir in sage, breadcrumbs, and egg. Use immediately, or transfer to an airtight container and refrigerate until ready to use.

INDEX

Apple and Almond Tartlets, 90
Apple and Spice Chicken, 74
Apple and Spice Muffins, 44
Apple Berry Crumble Cake, 84
Apple Champagne, 112
Apple Upside-Down Cake, 93
Applesauce, 122
  Apple Butter, 118
  Chestnut and Apple Soup, 12
asparagus
  Grilled Apple and Chicken Salad, 24
avocado
  Fruit and Nut Salad, 29
beets
  Beet, Feta, and Apple Soup, 17
  Roasted Apple and Beet Salad, 32
buttermilk
  Buttermilk Pancakes with Apples and Pecans, 102
carrots
  Apple Carrot Cake with Ginger Cream, 92
  Carrot and Apple Muffins, 50
  Carrot, Apple, and Ginger Soup, 14
  Chicken and Apple Tagine, 67
  Thai-Style Green Apple Salad, 35
celeriac
  Apple, Celery, and Celeriac Soup, 16
cheese
  Beet, Feta, and Apple Soup, 17
  Lemon Apple Cheesecake, 88
  Spicy Apple, Brie, and Rice Salad, 34
  Spinach, Apple, and Wheat Berry Salad, 26
chestnuts
  Chestnut and Apple Soup, 12
chocolate
  Apple Blondies, 52
  Chocolate Chip Apple Cookies, 40
  Chocolate-Coated Apple Cranberry Cookies, 58
chutney
  Mango-Apple Chutney, 116
  Classic Apple Chutney, 124
cider
  Apple Cider Dressing, 120

Apple Cider Sauce, 123
Apple Relish, 123
coconut cream
  Apple and Coconut Pudding, 100
  Carrot, Apple, and Ginger Soup, 14
cranberries
  Apple Muesli Cookies, 60
  Chocolate-Coated Apple Cranberry Cookies, 58
  Cranberry-Apple Loaf, 42
  Orange, Apple, and Cranberry Muffins, 49
  Quinoa and Apple Salad, 28
cranberry sauce
  Braised Beef with Red Wine, Cranberries, and Apples, 79
  Cranberry-Apple Chicken, 73
custard
  Apple Custard Tartlets, 94
  Mini Apple Custard Pots, 106
dates
  Apple and Date Loaf, 48
  Apple and Date Spice Cookies, 55
  Apple, Date, and Ginger Muffins, 54
  Simple Apple and Date Spread, 122
Easy Beef and Apple Curry, 78
fennel
  Roasted Chicken with Caramelized Fennel and Apples, 64
Fruity Hot Cider, 114
green beans
  Beef and Apple Stir-Fry, 70
lamb chops
  Lamb Chops with Caramelized Apples, Onions, and Mint, 76
lemon
  Apple, Lemon, and Poppy Seed Muffins with Mint Syrup, 46
  Apple, Lemon, and Yogurt Smoothie, 120
  Lemon Apple Cheesecake, 88
  Lemon, Apple, and Sage Grilled Chicken, 68
lentils
  Curried Apple Lentil Soup, 10
mango
  Fruit and Nut Salad, 29
  Mango-Apple Chutney, 116

meatballs
  Fruity Meatball Casserole, 72
Mini Apple Crisps, 98
Mini Toffee Apple Puddings, 104
muesli
  Apple Muesli Cookies, 60
mushrooms
  Mushroom, Sage, and Apple Stuffing, 126
oatmeal
  Apple Oatmeal Cookies, 56
oranges
  Apple Marmalade, 126
  Citrus Ginger Chicken, 66
  Warm Apple Wine, 112
pears
  Chilled Apple Soup, 13
  Pot Roast with Glazed Apple and Pears, 80
plums
  Apple and Plum Cake, 108
puff pastry
  Apple and Almond Tartlets, 90
  Easy Apple Strudel, 101
  Easy Tarte Tatin, 100
pumpkin
  Apple and Pumpkin Loaf, 40
  Country-Style Vegetable and Apple Soup, 21
  Grilled Apple and Chicken Salad, 24
  Pumpkin and Apple Soup 20
quinoa
  Quinoa and Apple Salad, 28
rice
  Beef and Apple Stir-Fry, 70
  Spicy Apple, Brie, and Rice Salad 34
Rustic Apple Cake, 86
sage
  Apple and Sage Burgers with Caramelized Onions, 72
  Lemon, Apple, and Sage Grilled Chicken, 68
  Mushroom, Sage, and Apple Stuffing, 126
salsa
  Apple Salsa, 114

shortcrust pastry
  Classic Apple Pie, 96
smoked salmon
  Smoked Salmon and Apple Salad, 30
smoothies
  Apple, Lemon, and Yogurt Smoothie, 120
  Apple, Pineapple, Ginger, and Mint Smoothie, 118
spinach
  Spinach, Apple, and Wheat Berry Salad, 26
strawberries
  Fruit and Nut Salad, 29
  Spinach, Apple, and Wheat Berry Salad, 26
stuffing
  Apricot, Apple, and Pecan Stuffing, 117
  Mushroom, Sage, and Apple Stuffing, 126
sweet potatoes
  Country-Style Vegetable and Apple Soup, 21
  Curried Apple Lentil Soup, 10
  Pumpkin and Apple Soup, 20
wasabi
  Apple, Chicken, and Wasabi Salad, 36
watercress
  Watercress and Apple Soup, 18
wheat berries
  Spinach, Apple, and Wheat Berry Salad, 26
wine
  Braised Beef with Red Wine, Cranberries, and Apples, 79
  Classic Apple Chutney, 124
  Pot Roast with Glazed Apple and Pears, 80
  Warm Apple Wine, 112
yogurt
  Apple and Coconut Pudding, 100
  Apple, Lemon, and Poppy Seed Muffins with Mint Syrup, 46
  Apple, Lemon, and Yogurt Smoothie, 120
  Chilled Apple Soup, 13